W9-BEH-992

-it as in sit

Kelly Doudna

Consulting Editor Monica Marx, M.A./Reading Specialist

Published by SandCastle™, an imprint of ABDO Publishing Company, 4940 Viking Drive, Edina, Minnesota 55435.

Printed in the United States.

Credits
Edited by: Pam Price
Curriculum Coordinator: Nancy Tuminelly
Cover and Interior Design and Production: Mighty Media
Photo Credits: BananaStock Ltd., Corbis Images, Eyewire Images, Hemera, PhotoDisc, Stockbyte

Library of Congress Cataloging-in-Publication Data

Doudna, Kelly, 1963-
    -It as in sit / Kelly Doudna.
        p. cm. -- (Word families. Set III)
        Summary: Introduces, in brief text and illustrations, the use of the letter combination "it" in such words as "sit," "split," "knit," and "outfit."
        ISBN 1-59197-240-X
        1. Readers (Primary) [1. Vocabulary. 2. Reading.] I. Title.

    PE1119 .D675845 2003
    428.1--dc21   2002038631

SandCastle™ books are created by a professional team of educators, reading specialists, and content developers around five essential components that include phonemic awareness, phonics, vocabulary, text comprehension, and fluency. All books are written, reviewed, and leveled for guided reading, early intervention reading, and Accelerated Reader® programs and designed for use in shared, guided, and independent reading and writing activities to support a balanced approach to literacy instruction.

Let Us Know

After reading the book, SandCastle would like you to tell us your stories about reading. What is your favorite page? Was there something hard that you needed help with? Share the ups and downs of learning to read. We want to hear from you! To get posted on the ABDO Publishing Company Web site, send us e-mail at:

sandcastle@abdopub.com

SandCastle Level: Beginning

-it Words

fit

kit

knit

outfit

sit

skit

Kim tries on the shirt to see if it will fit.

The paramedic has a
first-aid kit.

Mrs. Smith likes to knit.

Cindy has a special
holiday outfit.

Whit and his parents sit
on the grass.

Mick plays a clown in
a skit at school.

SPLIT!

My Outfit Split

SPLIT!

12

When I sat,
my pants split!

My outfit used to fit.

SLIT

But now there is a slit.

I have to wear
my outfit in a skit.

It starts in a little bit.

I don't know
how to knit.

I'll try to
fix my outfit
with a sewing kit.

I can't fix the split,
but I won't quit.

Instead, I'll wear
my new outfit.
It will be a hit!

The -it Word Family

bit	quit
fit	sit
it	skit
kit	slit
knit	spit
lit	split
outfit	Whit
pit	wit

Glossary

Some of the words in this list may have more than one meaning. The meaning listed here reflects the way the word is used in the book.

hit something popular or successful, such as a song or play

knit to connect loops of yarn or thread using needles

paramedic a person who provides emergency medical services before or during a trip to a hospital

skit a short performance, usually funny

special unusual or unique

split to tear or burst apart lengthwise

About SandCastle™

A professional team of educators, reading specialists, and content developers created the SandCastle™ series to support young readers as they develop reading skills and strategies and increase their general knowledge. The SandCastle™ series has four levels that correspond to early literacy development in young children. The levels are provided to help teachers and parents select the appropriate books for young readers.

Emerging Readers
(no flags)

Beginning Readers
(1 flag)

Transitional Readers
(2 flags)

Fluent Readers
(3 flags)

These levels are meant only as a guide. All levels are subject to change.

ABDO
Publishing Company

To see a complete list of SandCastle™ books and other nonfiction titles from ABDO Publishing Company, visit www.abdopub.com or contact us at:

4940 Viking Drive, Edina, Minnesota 55435 • 1-800-800-1312 • fax: 1-952-831-1632